POMPEII

A CITY FROZEN IN TIME

By Emily Costello

CELEBRATION PRESS

Pearson Learning Group

CONTENTS

VESUVIUS ERUPTS

August 24, A.D. 79, was an unusually hot day in Pompeii, a port city on the west coast of what is now Italy. Mount Vesuvius, a volcano about 6 miles away, was veiled in a strange, black cloud. Minor tremors from the mountain cracked walls and made animals behave strangely.

Still, about 20,000 residents went about their business. Workers repaired buildings, young boys studied **Latin**, girls practiced weaving cloth, and wealthy women and enslaved people visited the marketplace.

Meanwhile, pressure inside the mountain was building. Just after noon, an explosion too powerful to ignore jolted the town. The mountain's summit cracked open and began to glow a fiery red.

A huge amount of gas, **pumice**, and ash shot high into the air and blocked out the sun. A layer of ash began to fall on Pompeii. Then, tiny white pellets of pumice fell like hail, quickly piling up in the cobblestone streets and on **terra cotta** roofs.

Many townspeople tried to flee the strange and terrible storm. Some rushed from home without any of their possessions. Others tried to gather a few belongings.

The city gates were soon clogged with panicked crowds. Babies wailed and dogs barked. Parents clutched their children, covering their mouths and nose to protect them from the burning ash.

Once through the gates, most people headed away from the mountain, toward the coast. Many made it to their boat. However, as they tried to escape, a furious wind blew them back to shore.

For two days, pumice, ash, cinders, and rocks fell on Pompeii. **Earthquakes** rocked the town. Roofs collapsed. Poisonous gases seeped from the depths of the volcano.

On the second night, showers of ash spewed from the volcano. Superheated rock fell on Pompeii in the early morning. Anyone who was still alive died from the extreme heat. By the end of the second day, volcanic stone and ash completely covered Pompeii. Nearby, three small towns suffered the same awful fate.

Location of Mount Vesuvius

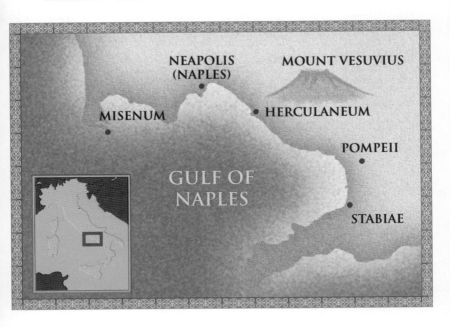

How do we know so much about this tragic day that took place nearly 2,000 years ago? **Archaeologists** have pieced together many clues. The **volcanologists** who studied Mount Vesuvius have also added information. Other details came directly from an eyewitness.

Pliny the Younger was the nephew of Pliny the Elder. The older man was an admiral in the Roman navy who lived in Misenum, a small town across the bay from Pompeii.

In A.D. 104, Pliny the Younger wrote two letters to the **historian** Tacitus, who lived in Rome. He described his experiences during the eruption of Vesuvius. From his uncle's home, Pliny the Younger could see a cloud shaped like an "umbrella pine." Then a messenger brought his uncle a plea for help from a friend who lived near Mount Vesuvius. Pliny the Younger wrote that his uncle "gave orders for the warships to be launched and went on board himself with the intention of bringing help to many."

Rough seas made it impossible for Pliny the Elder to dock his boat at Pompeii. One of his sailors advised turning back. However, Pliny told him "fortes fortuna iuvat." (That's Latin for "fortune favors the brave.")

This mosaic found in Pompeii shows what the city looked like before the eruption.

Pliny the Elder sailed on to Stabiae. There, he spent the night with a friend. By morning, they were experiencing earthquakes, falling pumice stones, and an ash storm. Pliny and his friend decided to flee the house. They went to the beach. There, Pliny the Elder died—probably from inhaling poisonous fumes.

More than 2,000 people lost their lives in Pompeii during the eruption of Vesuvius. Fortunately, about 18,000 were able to escape. Some of the survivors later returned to find their city buried beneath tons of cooling lava and ash.

The survivors tried to dig out their homes. They also attempted to rescue the bodies of loved ones. They gave up after cave-ins killed several people. Slowly, the survivors moved away and began their lives again elsewhere.

In time, grass sprouted on the slopes of Vesuvius. Farmers returned to the fertile land. Sheepherders came with their flocks. New towns were built near the buried city.

Years passed, and many people forgot about the ancient city. Some people told stories about the eruption, but nobody knew if the stories were true. More than 1,500 years passed before the sun shone again on the magnificent buildings and artwork of Pompeii.

The tragic eruption of Vesuvius created one of the most interesting places on Earth. Pompeii's ruins have much to tell about what life was like for the people who once made their home there.

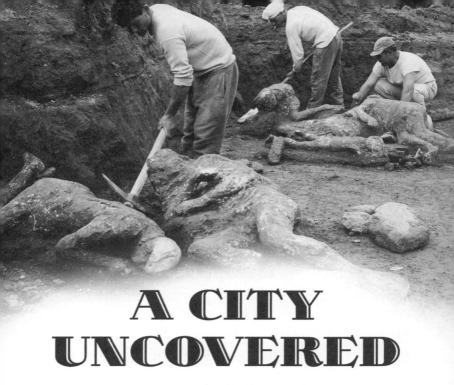

A CITY UNCOVERED

In 1594, workers building an underground **aqueduct** found ruined buildings. Amazingly, nobody paid much attention to the discovery. We now know that the workers had found part of Pompeii.

Then, in 1709, a well digger discovered a wall. This structure later turned out to be part of a theater in Herculaneum, a town near Pompeii. This time, people paid attention.

Treasure hunters dug tunnels through the porous rock. Their hard work paid off. They discovered ancient art and carried off anything that looked valuable.

At that time, modern Italy did not exist. The land near Vesuvius was part of the kingdom of Naples. Later in the 1700s, it fell under the leadership of a succession of French, Austrian, and Spanish kings.

In 1748, treasure hunters working for the king of Spain uncovered parts of ancient Pompeii. They carried off manuscripts, vases, jewelry, and more. Early **excavators** of Pompeii also found a tavern, several tombs, and a small theater. In 1772, diggers found 18 bodies in an underground passage.

By the 1780s, the ruins had become popular with tourists. Writers visited Pompeii and wrote about their experiences. The ancient city's fame grew. Scholars began to complain about plundering.

Then, in 1861, the Vesuvius region became part of the new country of Italy. An archaeologist named Giuseppe Fiorelli took control of Pompeii. Fiorelli developed a careful plan for excavating the buried city. He kept records of what was found and where he found it. Fiorelli's system is still used today.

Fiorelli also created a way to study Pompeii's victims. Over the centuries, the buried bodies rotted away and left empty spaces in the hard volcanic ash. The features of the bodies were preserved in the hardened ash. Fiorelli filled the empty spaces with plaster. After the plaster set, he carefully chipped the ash away.

This cast shows an unlucky dog that was buried in ash. You can still see its collar!

Fiorelli's casts reveal amazing details. From them, we've learned how Pompeians wore their hair and what kind of clothes they liked. Some casts even show facial expressions. One shows a dog that struggled to escape before it was buried in ash.

Unlocking the secrets of Pompeii is important because Pompeii was a small part of a great civilization, the Roman Empire. The Roman Empire has greatly affected our own language and customs. The Romans also influenced our form of government and laws.

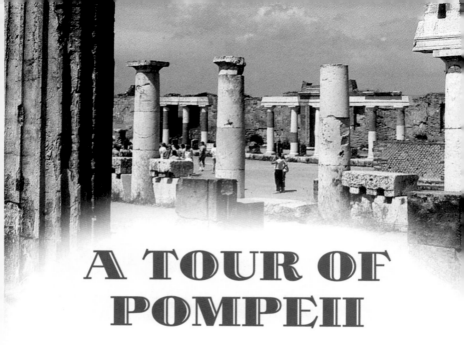

A TOUR OF POMPEII

The Roman Empire was enormous. At one time, it stretched from Spain to Syria and from Britain down to Egypt. Pompeii was a typical Roman city of the time. It had a forum, public baths, **temples** dedicated to various gods, and an **amphitheater**.

The forum was the commercial, political, and religious center of a Roman town. The forum was more like a city square. It was enclosed on three sides by two-story **colonnades**.

Trials took place in the **basilica**. Large events were held in the amphitheater. Pompeii's merchants held a daily market in the forum. There, people bought sandals, got haircuts, ate, did business, or met friends.

The rich people of Pompeii ate bread, olives, olive oil, cheese, fruit, fish, and exotic meats. They enjoyed dinner parties that lasted for hours. Poor people did not have place to cook at home. They had to buy hot meals from stalls in the street.

One of Pompeii's specialties was garum. Vendors made this strong-smelling sauce by fermenting fish, olive oil, and herbs in the sun for three days. Pompeians used garum to flavor their food.

The walls of Pompeii's buildings are still covered with ancient graffiti. These markings advertise goods that were for sale, announce gladiator fights in the amphitheater, and promote political candidates who were up for election. Archaeologists study this graffiti to learn about social life in Pompeii.

Pompeii's attractions included an amphitheater, a forum, and cobblestone streets.

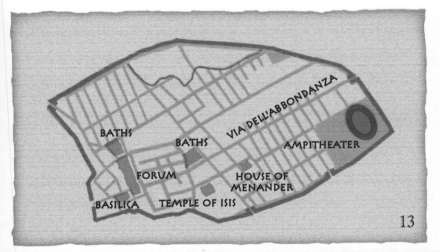

13

THE BATHS

Pompeii had three baths that were like modern health clubs. The citizens of Pompeii went to the baths daily. Separate sections of the baths were designed for men and women.

A visit might have begun with some exercise, such as wrestling, running, or weight lifting. Next, citizens visited the tepidarium, or warm bath. Here, enslaved people massaged the patrons with oil and then scraped their bodies clean with curved pieces of metal.

Once they were clean, the patrons moved on to the caldarium, or hot bath, for a long soak. Before leaving, they cooled off with a quick dip into a cold pool called the frigidarium.

What might have been the finishing touch? Perhaps it was another massage with scented oils and a snack from one of the busy shops surrounding the baths.

A visit to the baths may have taken several hours, but the baths were not only a place to exercise and get clean. They were also a place to hear the news of the day and to share gossip with friends. Poets recited their work there, and musicians performed.

THE GODS

Religion was important to the Pompeians. The people built grand temples and household shrines to their gods. Infants received special good luck charms called bullas and wore them until adulthood.

The citizens believed that the gods looked after different parts of life. The goddess Venus was believed to protect Pompeii. People also worshiped Hercules, Bacchus, and the Egyptian goddess Isis.

Most people feared the gods and tried to keep them happy by giving them gifts. If things went poorly, they believed the gods were angry. What must they have thought when Vesuvius erupted?

The Temple of Isis at Pompeii

THE AMPHITHEATER

Battles between wild bears! Lions hunting gazelles! Gladiators doing battle! The public amusements enjoyed in Pompeii were dramatic and often bloody.

Gladiators were something like the wrestlers of today—except that they often fought to the death. Many were enslaved people or prisoners of war who were forced to fight. Others were freedmen attracted by prize money.

Gladiators had special styles. Some were dressed in heavy armor, with swords and a helmet. Others fought using only a net. Umpires watched the battles and enforced rules, much like umpires do in present times.

Gladiators fought in a huge arena called an amphitheater. The amphitheater in Pompeii seated 20,000 people. It had a seat for every man, woman, and child in town.

The building itself was amazing. Its designers built it up against one of the city walls. It had stairs and ramps for the spectators and a special corridor that was probably used for removing dead animals and men.

Gladiators in battle

Not all the shows in the amphitheater were bloody. Events such as plays and circuses were also held in a typical Roman amphitheater.

In A.D. 59, the amphitheater in Pompeii was the site of a riot. The fight was sparked when fans from a nearby town exchanged insults with the citizens of Pompeii. Stones were thrown, and swords were drawn! Fans from both sides were killed. Officials in Rome reacted by closing the amphitheater for ten years.

LIFE IN POMPEII

A few lucky residents of Pompeii were very rich. They lived in grand houses with running water. They owned art, silver dishes, and gold jewelry. They decorated their homes with wall paintings and floor **mosaics**. Enslaved people saw to their every need.

Less fortunate residents of the city lived in modest apartments above stores. They had to haul fresh water from public fountains. Residents without sewer connections dumped their sewage and garbage into the street. It remained there until the rain washed it away.

THE HOUSE OF MENANDER

The House of Menander is one of the most famous buildings in Pompeii. It is also one of the most popular places to visit. The house had private baths, a large shrine, and many mosaics and paintings.

The house's name comes from a famous portrait of the ancient Greek poet Menander. The portrait is painted on one of the walls surrounding the courtyard.

Many interesting objects have been found in the House of Menander. They include portraits of hunting scenes, a carved silver cup, a golden bulla, coins, jewelry, and worker's materials.

The worker's materials, found piled in the garden, show that the house was probably being remodeled when Vesuvius erupted. Workers might have been repairing damage caused by an earthquake that struck the city in A.D. 62.

The House of Menander held many treasures, including this silver cup.

ROMAN SOCIETY

Pompeii had a highly organized society. People were either enslaved, freedmen, or citizens. Nearly half of the people living in Pompeii were enslaved. Some of them were prisoners of war or had enslaved parents.

Enslaved people had no rights or privileges. They performed the hardest jobs, such as working in the fields, making garum, and minding the fires that kept the baths warm. A few well-educated enslaved people worked as craftspeople, doctors, or tutors.

Occasionally, a Roman citizen would grant freedom to a loyal slave. A few lucky enslaved people managed to buy their freedom. Freedmen's children became Roman citizens.

Citizens could vote in elections and had access to the best jobs. They also had special responsibilities. They had to serve in the army and pay taxes.

Citizens were divided into two classes: patricians and plebeians. Patricians were the wealthiest and held the most important jobs. Equites, a class of patricians, were merchants. Ordinary citizens were called plebeians.

Some women in Pompeii were employed as weavers, nurses, or musicians. Others helped their husbands or took care of the house and children.

A young husband and wife from Pompeii

Girls married young, around age 13. Their parents tried to find them husbands who were rich or powerful. Once a marriage was arranged, the girl's parents paid a **dowry** of clothes, money, and goods to the groom's family.

Boys married later. However, they didn't have much more control over their lives than girls. The occupations they could enter were decided by their family's wealth and power.

The son of a shopkeeper often learned his father's trade. Other trades in Pompeii included potter, coppersmith, silversmith, goldsmith, glass blower, carpenter, and mason.

The Roman Empire was built by a powerful military.

Wealthier boys were well educated. They learned Latin, Greek, math, philosophy, and public speaking. These subjects prepared them for a career such as politics.

Many young men became soldiers. Both citizens and noncitizens were encouraged to join the army. Citizens became legionaries. Noncitizens were called auxiliaries.

Joining the army was a big decision. When people signed up, it was for 25 years. At the end of their service, auxiliaries were given citizenship. Retired soldiers were paid a pension.

Each soldier was heavily armed. He carried two javelins, a short sword, and a shield made of wood and leather. Soldiers wore metal helmets, short armor vests, woolen **tunics**, and metal leg protectors. Their sandals were reinforced with long-lasting knobbed nails because soldiers often marched long distances carrying heavy loads.

Being a soldier was difficult work. Training was hard, and discipline was strict. The punishment for desertion was death. That could explain why the body of a soldier was found near one of Pompeii's gates. He apparently feared the power of the Roman army more than the fury of Mount Vesuvius.

The writer Mark Twain visited Pompeii and was moved by the soldier's story. In a book published in 1875, he wrote, "True to his proud name of a soldier of Rome . . . [he] stood to his post by the city gate."

A soldier's sandals

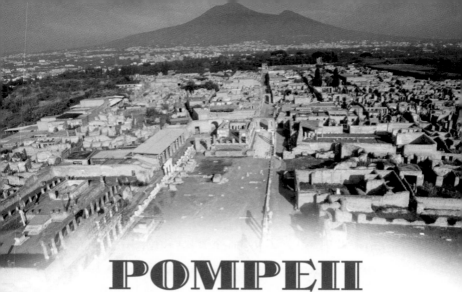

POMPEII TODAY

Digging up Pompeii has allowed scholars to learn about how ancient Romans lived. However, it exposed the treasures of Pompeii to serious dangers. Sunlight fades paintings. Wind and rain damage ancient plaster on buildings. In November 1980, a strong earthquake weakened the structures even more.

People cause most of the damage to the sites. Some of the destruction is done innocently. Thousands of footsteps passing over the ancient sidewalks cause them to crumble. A visitor might not realize that touching a piece of mosaic may loosen it.

Sadly, other people are destructive on purpose. They scribble their names on ancient paintings, or they make a game out of knocking over columns. In the past, the Italian government seemed unable to stop this vandalism. Today, however, the government is trying to prevent it.

Today, Mount Vesuvius is one of the most dangerous volcanoes on Earth. It has erupted dozens of times since A.D. 79. In 1631, an eruption claimed about 4,000 lives. Alarmingly, many people still live near the volcano. About 26,000 people make their home in Pompeii. More than 1 million people live in the nearby city of Naples.

Experts say hundreds of thousands of people could be killed by a modern-day eruption of Vesuvius. So, why do so many people live in the volcano's shadow?

There is a real danger that Mount Vesuvius might erupt again.

People love living in Naples because of the area's natural beauty. Mount Vesuvius is part of the lovely scenery. Another reason people want to live in the area is the soil. Farmers use the rich soil near Mount Vesuvius to grow fruits and vegetables.

The people there may also believe volcanologists will warn them of an eruption in time for them to get away. Volcanologists are not sure that it is possible to do this.

Naples is not the only city thriving near a deadly volcano. One volcanologist calls volcanoes "people magnets."

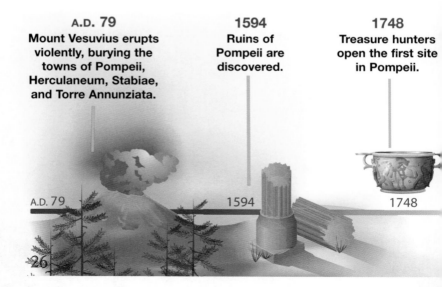

A.D. 79
Mount Vesuvius erupts violently, burying the towns of Pompeii, Herculaneum, Stabiae, and Torre Annunziata.

1594
Ruins of Pompeii are discovered.

1748
Treasure hunters open the first site in Pompeii.

A.D. 79

1594

1748

Researchers recently counted the number of areas where 1 million or more people live near a volcano. They found 457! One, Mexico City, Mexico, has a population of more than 20 million people who live less than 50 miles from a volcano.

Just like many modern cities, Pompeii was once a vital bustling city in the shadow of a volcano. Today, many people are curious about what Pompeii was like. They want to know what happened to it so long ago. However, the story is still incomplete because the digging and the research continue. There is still much to learn about the city that was frozen in time.

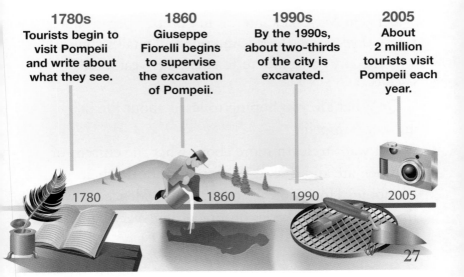

1780s
Tourists begin to visit Pompeii and write about what they see.

1860
Giuseppe Fiorelli begins to supervise the excavation of Pompeii.

1990s
By the 1990s, about two-thirds of the city is excavated.

2005
About 2 million tourists visit Pompeii each year.

1780   1860   1990   2005

WORDS OF A HISTORIAN

Betty Jo Mayeske's interest in Pompeii began more than 30 years ago. In this interview, she talks about why the city continues to fascinate her year after year.

Q: What are you hoping to learn about life in ancient Pompeii?

A: I want to learn more about what the citizens of Pompeii ate and drank. Where did they do their shopping? How did they cook? The evidence shows that there were bakeries on practically every block.

Q: What do you enjoy about being at this special site?

A: I especially love the bakeries with their mills, counters, and ovens. One oven had 80 loaves of nearly 2,000-year-old bread inside. The loaves are round and scored into eight sections. Bread made in Pompeii today still has a similar shape.

Q: Do we know what the bread tasted like?

A: Well, several authors have said that rich people ate white bread and poor people ate brown bread.

Q: How is your study unique?

A: Unlike most researchers, we're surveying aspects of food and drink in the entire 157-acre city.

Q: If you had three wishes for Pompeii, what would they be?

A: One, I'd like more money spent to preserve valuable structures, prevent theft, and deal with environmental issues. Two, I'd like more historians to undertake surveys like mine. I think we need to coordinate the information we already have about Pompeii. Three, I'd like to know that Mount Vesuvius won't erupt again, because it's a very dangerous volcano.

This bread is almost 2,000 years old!

Did You Know?

- A volcano is an opening in Earth's surface through which ash, gas, and liquid rock from deep within the Earth erupt.

- Scientists have counted about 1,500 active volcanoes on Earth.

- Seven huge plates make up Earth's crust. Volcanoes tend to form in places where these plates come together.

- Mauna Loa is the largest volcano in the world. It is located on the island of Hawaii.

- Most volcanologists put Mount Vesuvius on their list of most dangerous volcanoes because it has a history of deadly activity, and a large population lives nearby.

Mauna Loa is the world's largest volcano.

- The eruption of Mount Vesuvius in A.D. 79 wasn't the deadliest eruption ever. About ten eruptions have killed more people.

- An 1815 eruption at Mount Tambora took about 92,000 lives.

- In 1883, an eruption of Mount Krakatau created a tidal wave that drowned about 36,000 people. Both Mount Tambora and Mount Krakatau are in Indonesia.

- There are active volcanoes in the United States.

- The most recent volcano that erupted in the continental United States was Mount St. Helens in Washington.

- Many volcanologists consider Mount Rainier near Seattle to be the most dangerous volcano

GLOSSARY

amphitheater   an oval or circular building, similar to a stadium, used for games or performances

aqueduct   a channel that carries water into a city or estate

archaeologists   people who study past human life by examining fossils and objects left behind

basilica   a public meeting place in ancient Rome

colonnades   evenly spaced rows of columns, often supporting a roof

dowry   property a woman brings to her husband at marriage

earthquakes   vibrations, sometimes violent, in the Earth's crust

excavators   people who uncover something by digging

historian   an expert or writer of history

Latin   the language of the Roman Empire

mosaics   designs or pictures made by joining together small pieces of stone or glass

pumice   light volcanic rock or glass with small holes in it, like a hardened sponge

temples   buildings used for worship

terra cotta   a hard, reddish-brown clay used as a building material

tunics   knee-length, sleeveless outer garments

volcanologists   scientists who study volcanoes